First and Last Words

First
and Last
Words

Poems by

FRED CHAPPELL

Louisiana State University Press
Baton Rouge and London
1989

98 97 96 95 94 93 92 91 90 89   5 4 3 2 1

Designer: Albert Crochet
Typeface: Linotron Palatino
Typesetter: G&S Typesetters, Inc.
Printer: Thomson-Shore, Inc.
Binder: John H. Dekker & Sons, Inc.

LIBRARY OF CONGRESS CATALOGING-IN-PUBLICATION DATA
Chappell, Fred, 1936–
    First and last words : poems / by Fred Chappell.
        p.   cm.
    ISBN 0-8071-1486-3 (cloth). ISBN 0-8071-1487-1
(pbk.: alk. paper)
    I. Title.   II. Title: 1st and last words.
PS3553.H298F57 1989
811'.54—dc19
                                            88-22041
                                                CIP

The paper in this book meets the guidelines for permanence and
durability of the Committee on Production Guidelines for Book
Longevity of the Council on Library Resources. ∞

Many of these poems have seen prior publication in the
following periodicals: *Abatis* (University of Tampa), *America,
Amicus Journal, Appalachian Heritage, Archive, Arts Journal,
Boulevard, Carolina Quarterly, Chariton Review, Chronicles, Coraddi,
Cream City Review, Denver Quarterly, Film Journal, Georgia Review,
Hemlocks and Balsams, Publication of the Society for Literature and
Science, St. Andrews Review, Tar River Poetry, Virginia Quarterly
Review.*

"Afternoons with Allen" and "The Gift To Be Simple" were
published as broadsides by Stuart Wright at Palaemon Press.

"A Prayer for the Hanged Man" was published in broadside by
Robert Denham at Iron Mountain Press.

Contents

Contents

Epilogues

Poem Dedicatory
to Mr. Reynolds Price

To what mentor shall I send
This book the eraser could not quite mend?
Reynolds, to you; who, decades gone,
Encouraged my work almost alone;
You, the artist in our group
Who first succeeded and gave us hope—
This book is yours. May the Muse
Find it ever of some small use.

—after Catullus

Prologues

An Old Mountain Woman Reading the Book of Job

The veiny wrist, the knobby finger-joints,
The scar-creased palm, the thumb she lifts to wet
And lift the corner of the memoried page,
Turning once more through Job's bewilderment:
What histories are written into her hand . . .

Aforetime she was as a tabret, but now
They change the night to day, the light is short,
The world delivered to ungodly shadow.
The darkness of her hand darkens the page.
She straightens her bifocals in which the words,
Reflected, jitter, then come to rest like moths.
It is November. The woodstove shifts its log
And grumbles. The night is longer than her fire.

She moves her lips to read but does not speak.
What is there to answer to the terrible words,
To these sharp final words that engrave the fate
Of a hammered old man? She sees the man
As if he stood before her, torn from the storm
Of time to be her husband, her dead husband.
She knows the man as man, his house and fields
Up Jarvis Creek going down in sawbriar,
The doctor bills chewing the farm like locusts.
Bleak Job scourged ceaseless in the starless night,
Her husband made holy by lean ravishment:
The whirlwind-savage hand of God forecloses
The mortgage; the fields are auctioned clod by clod,
The skies are auctioned cloud by pallid cloud.

The Book of Job draws all its shadow over
Her thumbed-limp Bible. St. Paul does not escape,
Not even Jesus shines clear of Job tonight,
The darkness of that blindly punished lament.
Shall any teach God knowledge?   —But if He knows;
And still permits . . . There is a weeping madness
In the thought she tries so feebly to push away.
Her trust lies down in dirt like a fractured tower.

Everything shall be restored, the Book
Tells her. But why should it be taken away?
Or given in the first place? Her husband Charles,
The man she knows as Job, mild unto death,
She doubts will be restored. The Book of Job
Distills to salt in the tear that seals her eye.

Let her then go out on Ember Mountain,
And cry out in his stead and say those words
She shall imagine for him, imagining
Herself there in the dark, in pitiless wind,
Raising her old fist to dare the lightning
And the gates of wrath, herself alone in wind
And saying the words that God's wind lacerates.
Let it be her there stricken, blasted, shriveled
Like a candlewick, and not the man
Her husband, whom the Lord like a hunting lion
Has carried off, her Job who suffered silence
As he went down never to rise again.

That silence does not yield. Her vision tears;
She never shall curse God, she never shall
Climb Ember Mountain again, nor ever weep.

But then she feels a throb in this old house
In which she sits alone, nursing her fire,
Her fear. A tremor as of someone walking
In another room, the kitchen or cold bedroom.
Someone unfamiliar is walking there,
Someone no kin to her, maybe no friend,
Who comes to bring her tidings the dead have risen
And all the wholeness of the earth brought back.
She holds her breath till the phantom goes away.

She shuts the Book of Job. She will not suffer
A God Who suffers the suffering of man,
Who sends the fatherless their broken arms,
Who sends away the widows empty as faith.
Tonight's no night for the heartless bedside prayer.

The Watchman

a prologue to the *Oresteia*

The watchman keeps his vigil on the roof
Of the ruining house. This long year,
Stretched out on his belly like a hound,
He has awaited the semaphore
Blaze, awaited proof
Of the victory that shall pull down
A proud and bitter family. In rain
Or cold starshine, gripping the eave,
He has searched the hard horizon for a sign.

A thirst is in him for the triumph of his king.
A rage is in his nation to know
They shall not know disgrace,
Shall not bow
Their heads before an alien race
And barbarous gods. Though the prophets sing
A deeper tragedy to follow—
Exile, homicide, treachery—
The city still must celebrate its victory.

He is fatigued with longing. The mountain peak
He stares toward, beyond the sleeping thorps
And dewy pastures, seems to advance and recede,
Dark against the dark.
The stars flitter stupidly overhead
Like an irritated squad of flies above a corpse.

Shall he still recognize
The signal? So many hours,
So many nights of silent skies
Have darkened his capacities
To comprehend. The arrow showers
Of meteors no longer startle; he no longer numbers
The familiar constellation stars.
The Great Bear lumbers
Over his spirit, leaving a shadow like a mortal bruise.

—But what is that? A signal light?
A reflected glimmer of dawning sun,

7

Or only a trick of exhausted eyesight?
Awake awake awake awake!

The murderous birth of justice has begun.

Patience

a prologue to *The Georgics*

1

An early summer evening.
Of the hive of stars immerses the dark porches where
The farmers muse. It seems that all the earth there is
Has been taken by the plow, and the hedgy boundaries
Of orchards encroach upon the sea, all the sea
There is, the planet lapped in grateful breathing fields:
Here the labor is, here the finished work.

Night blackens the red ox in his pen, the roan horse
Shines like the dust of galaxies: our faithful creatures—
For whom time is a patience almost mineral,
Whose sleep this evening folds over like a loamy furrow—
Snort, and settle to the ground like velvet boulders;
And ivy in the night curls up about them bronze.

The farmers and their animals have sculpted the world
To a shape like some smooth monumental family group,
The father mountains and the mother clouds, their progeny meadows
Stationed about them, as if posing for a photograph
To be taken from a silver orbiter spaceship by beings
Like angelic horses, who return to their home world
With pleasant report: *Leave Earth alone, it is at peace.*

2

Always the Poet knew it wasn't that way.
War throughout the globe, justice and injustice
Confounded, every sort of knavery, the plow
Disused unhonored, the farmer conscripted and his scythe
Straitly misshapen to make a cruel sword.
Imbrued, and northern Europe, and all the smaller tribes
Ceaselessly breaking their treaties, and Mars the infidel
Savages every field. The shepherd and the herdsman,
Et robustus item curvi moderator aratri,
And the muscular steersman of the crooked plow, are killed,

The cottager mothers flung on the corpses of their children . . .
As when the horses seize the bit from the chariot-driver
And thunder over the circus barrier into the crowd,
He jerks the useless reins, the car will not respond.

3

Such slaughter, they say, manures the fields of Utopia.
So that the plowman in a sleepier century
Turns up the bones of a legendary Diomedes
And marvels that the land used to nourish those giants
Who have now become the subsoil in which the Capitol
Is footed; where the softhanded senators daylong
Argue the townsman's ancient case against the farmer:
He is behind the times, he will never understand.
The decisions there brought back to the homestead in the form of taxes
And soldiers, who look with envious eyes upon this life
They fleer at, guzzling the murky raw-edged country wine.

But nothing changes. The war grinds over the world and all
Its politics, the soldiers marry the farmers' daughters
And tell their plowman sons about the fight at the Scaean Gate,
And the other sanguine braveries the dust has eaten.
Sundown still draws the chickens to their purring roost,
The cow to the milking stall, the farmer to his porch to watch
Whether the soaring constellations promise rain.

Legions

a prologue to Livy

Opening now again unopening, the mountain
mantles its forest with cloud. The heavens
and earth conjoin, cumulus
of pines and rock, the sky the foraging deer
shine in like little pulses of thunder.

An infantry climbs toward the invisible pass,
making slow time. As if ascending
a ladder of painful virtues. Gleam
of blades and helmets rises through
the mist, silence

blots them from sight, the tumid oblivion
of cloud and grove receives them
forever, like the embrace of a dying father.
They have been ordered to engage
their destiny of smoke.

Tolstoy's Bear

Disgusting Russia, he told his diary,
Russia is abysmal; set down new Rules
Of Life: *Avoid the gaming table; rise early.*
Benjamin Franklin remained his adorable saint.
Eager and restless, he hung up his sword
And St. Anne's medal. *A thousand vanities . . .*

And saddled the famous horse that made him weep,
Gathered the glossy hounds, and sped to the forest
To make his presence known to the towering bear
Who mauled him promptly. His rifle had missed fire.
Then: Hugger-mugger in the autumn ferns
The monsters embraced for love of the fury of life.
The beaters could not say who was the man
In the cozy tumult. The bear hung on for madness,
The Count was given "a vision of crisp blue sky
Framed sharply by the bright green tossing treetops."
This vision nearly cost the man his eye;
He found it in the bear's wounded open mouth.

It was a peasant with his cudgel drove off
The bear galumphing like a creditor
Into the woods. Tolstoy rose and vowed
A better life, new theories, harder Rules.

Four days later he returned to kill his bear,
And had it skinned and spread on the study floor
Where he could keep a soulful eye upon it;
Marched barefoot up and down, writing his novels.

An early winter descended like silver blindness
As the Count pawed over his Russian cruelties.

Meanwhile

a prologue to *The Death of Ivan Ilych*

A man must get ahead in the world.
He must kiss, in prescribed and ancient order,
the lipworn arses of his goldplate ministry
superiors. It is a form of prayer,

he feels. Because the man who gets ahead
must show his piety, must hang the costly drapes
of burgundy velvet in the sitting room. . . .
The house plunges its spear into his side.

At midnight in the paneled library he pours
a brandy and tries to think about his life.
He ponders instead his career which gleams
like a samovar. Now he is tired, dull pain

beneath his heart, he must begin
a sensible diet tomorrow. Meanwhile, picquet.
Meanwhile, gossip and roast veal. Meanwhile,
meanwhile. Death pays an informal call

and they talk for an hour, but the words are banal.
He explains that he is merely ordinary,
a man of middle rank, he had not expected
a visitor so distinguished. The torture

is that it never felt like torture, the horror
is that it was always ordinary always.
A man must get ahead in the world,
the world that breaks its first and only promise.

Stoic Poet

a prologue to *The Dynasts*

The sun's regret, the sorrow of the moon
have suffered him. He works the dark,
he mines the nighttime.
He gains a knowledge would cause an easy man
to embitter and grow lean.
Terrors assail him, he holds steady,
absorbing the wounds of the world's every crime:
a spirit who might teach the stars to mourn,
our stars implacable and indifferent.
He has filatured his human sympathies
until they tremble delicate and resilient
as the wind that throbs across the glacier ice,
the shining mindless wind that glistens the distant
tribes of islands in their barbarian seas.

The Gift To Be Simple

a prologue to Aaron Copland's *Appalachian Spring*

O Music is that Valley of love and delight
Where Day turns on Day, Night turns on Night,
And looking clear about us, we genially see
A natural transparent Open Harmony.

For Music is Order, and Order we have found
Is of all Sane Things the sanest and most sound,
And to live close within it we must straiten our Lives,
Enlighten our dear Children, and cherish our sweet Wives.

For we have it within us to bow and to bend
To the Order within us that is our True Friend;
For Order is a Music of such health and delight
That in hearing it newly we come round right.

Afternoons with Allen

a prologue to *The Fathers*

He'd smilingly admit, with M. Teste,
"Stupidity is not my long suit." Then
Intently turn his pale pale eyes upon
Lombardi's Redskins mauling the TV screen.

"It's their precision I like, like a machine,"
He said, "like well made poetry." And when
They lost he didn't much appear to care,
But chuckled at the unimportant score.

"Kicking is still part of the game. I'm glad."
He took a sip of meditative bourbon
And lit a cigarette. "Please don't tell Helen
I've been smoking."
                              (We didn't; but felt we should.)

Like Homer's famous snowflakes his words drifted
In the brass October brunt of light. He lifted
And let fall his delicate hand of smoke
That winged, moth-hesitant, through all his talk.

Tracery, traceries . . . Sometimes there stood outlined
Before us, features of a remembered friend.
"Hem thought we make love just so many times;
A hot youth means short rations at the end.

"Miss Stein I never liked, rude, ignorant,
And prejudiced. I always wondered why
No one saw through her. Toklas was merely
Sad. Pound's talent crumbed into rant.

"My southern friends have been the best to me
Even when we fell out." For Lombardi
He fetched out of that high magniloquent head
A telling line of the Second Aeneid.

Forsitan et, Priami fuerint quae fata, requiras?

Entr'acte

My Hand Placed on a Rubens Drawing

1

It is what it is,
And being what it is, is something more
Than its wrinkle, thumb, and knobble indicate.
The lumpy knuckles, nails chipped and pitted,
Gross pores, ashen stipple of keratin spots,
Little scars with forgotten histories:
My hand no uglier than another man's
Middle-aged, luckless, but not brutal hand,
Expressing a studied inexpressiveness.

So much a part of my world, it is my world

And cannot enter the one the scholars have named
Study of a Woman with Crossed Hands,
A world that Rubens with some thousand strokes
Has set in motion and then set at rest.

My hand placed on the drawing, that universe
So overflooded with its single dream.
Both worlds intransigent as never before,
Their transit far and darkling.
                                        Not a shadow
My hand throws on the page; a spirit rises,
Antique and cool, out of the page to touch
My hand. And then recoils. Returns inside
Its nest of scrawlwork, blot and thoughtful smear.
My unacknowledged hand lifts slowly backward:
I am become alien to myself.

Myself a stranger to myself.
                                    The gods
Affect us in just this way: passing by
Heedlessly, absorbed by what can absorb
Divinities, they tremble the human earth
Like marble temples falling one by one.
They are close enough; it is enough
To think they once created the history,

Unmoving star-scarp pitiless,
The history that now rejects my hand.

2

Woman with Crossed Hands

Not the usual Rubens woman.
That is,
Not one of his grand horsy Venuses
Who has donned a robe of opalescent flesh
The way she might step into royal ermine
For the painter's convenience; splendidly clothed
In splendid nudity, big pearly dumpling
Who embodies longing's sleekest fulfillment. . . .
Not one of those.
A younger woman. Drifting,
Just now having drifted, into a trance
Of shadowed reverie. Lips barely parted,
The gaze affectionate, fixed upon
Some object the pencil and chalk have left undrawn.
A figure for an Adoration, perhaps,
A quiet figure not less joyful because
Rubens for once is not sounding the whole
Outsized orchestra of Flemish flesh,
The tuba bellies and thighs, kettledrum buttocks,
The pale blonde appogiatura breasts.

She is chamber music, intimate
Though a little withdrawn, modestly
Intoning a demure contralto line.

She is entranced. She was going to smile,
And then forgot. Something came over her—
A sybilline moment, a daydream peek
Into a happy future, warm, unhurried,
Maternal, graceful. Eyes smudged with joys foreseen.

The face *incipient;* it will blossom,
Some future moment, into a various garden
Of expression: coquettries, giggles, kisses, frowns;
She will unveil the smile she forgot to smile.

The hands, however, are an accomplished event;
Like my own hands, they are what they are.
Graceful but never noble, they tell the story
Of farmer ancestry, staunch country forebears,
And contradict in some small measure the easy
Fine bearing of the head. Thoroughly modeled,
They emerge from the blouse-cuff—cascade of scribble,
Ebullient froth of marking—as Venus rose
Out of the sea foam whole and ready as sunlight.
The smell of earth about them, undertone
Of cabbage, onion, potato, the branmeal loaf.

Rubens sinks the piers of vision deep
Into the earth, secures the billowed gods
And hurtling towers, the saints and babes and heroes—
All that panoply of gleaming triumph—
With her hands the paring knife and grater
Have sculpted to simple peace and simple welcome.

                3

  The ages work toward mastery
  Of a single gesture. A torso's twist,
  The revelation of a thigh,
  White stone corded in a fist:

  Fragments that might still add up
  To compose a figure of the perfected soul
  As it releases from the grip
  Of vision that burned to draw it whole.

Voyagers

after Vermeer's *The Astronomer*

The scholar and his globe celestial,
His book that names the fixed and ambling stars,
Their ascensions, declinations, appointed seasons:

Hic pinxit. In this dim room that admits no more
Of Delft than its refined gray window-light,
This room that silence studies like a science,

The scholar and his celestial globe commerce.
He turns the globe, he turns the pages, the silver
Little pages that speak in pillars of numbers

Of when the homesick sea captain first glimpsed
Centaurus in the southern latitudes
And wrote the name of it and the lonesome hour.

The dagger coast of Tierra del Fuego
Discloses fjord by fjord itself as the pages
Turn, the scholar and his whirligig

Agree. The oceans after all agree
With what the astronomer tells the stars to do
From his room at Delft with his little silver book.

Pierrot Escapes

1

He floats. The triple gibbet of paradise
Flees into gray distance. The tufted clouds
Graze like salmon-colored sheep in the blue
And sunless sky. Below him prairies of mandolins

Glitter like oceans of porcelain marguerites,
Their song a smoky echo. Pierrot is busy
With his ropes and gauges, pensive
As ever, a pale interior man. The world

He leaves behind, all that pastoral chat and clatter,
He begins to remember in the way that one recalls
The scent of the crushed clover of childhood.
His balloon sways him like a pendulum.

2

Far from the carnival of noble hearts, he wanders
Shining like a butterfly, far
From the fresh and fragile brilliance, that light
Transforming folly into figures of a dance.

The sky surrounds him with fretful angels
Of whom he takes no note. *O my sisters,*
What was it all about, that life petite
And nougat? The chandeliers are falling,

The ivied garden tiers collapse, an avalanche
Of frou-frou buries the searching mind. Pierrot,
Balloonist and philosopher, considers
His escape with a lonely satisfaction. No more,

3

No more of that forever. *Untie the garter ribband*
Of society. Farewell farewell
The coifed spaniel and bal masqué. Pierrot's balloon
Rises among the stars like a wedding cake.

Slow Harbor

The seas draw the autumn over them.
The long night heaps such wealth of stars
That lovers in the harbor town
Snuff their lamps, take in the fretwork sky
As if entering once more a childhood.

They raise their faces toward Polaris.
The cathedral of starlight
Settles upon the town like a butterfly,
Silent and tensible, unfolding its brilliant
Symmetries.   That is how it is:

Star-cathedral that slides upon the town,
As lovers slide upon one another,
Cheek and thigh and shoulder, almost
Touchless.
                The onset they cannot recognize
Of winter, the early light like snow.

A Prayer for the Hanged Man

Sunset bares its bronze thigh behind
the swaying gibbet, the wind in the copse
of ravens swims toward the mountain.
She is cutting her brother down, the rope
as deep into his neck as a coil of acids.

Let no prayer come to her then, no phrase
that lights her like a bronze sunset. Let
there be hard weight in her like a brother's
stiffened legs, a sorrow like the slow gray
glisten of the hangman's Sunday, let there be
fury as patient and certain as the birth of stone.

Bee

The house is changed where death has come,
as the rose is changed
by the visit of the bee and his freight of pollen.
The house is opened to the mercies
of strangers to whom the dead father
is presented like a delectable veal,
for whom the linens are unearthed
and spread to air, the whiskies decanted.

Survivors gossip their last respects:
a bumble of voices in the living room
                like the drowse of music
around the white hive busy in the sunny field.

In the breathless upstairs bedroom,
                one lost bee
crawls the pane behind the glass curtain,
searching to enter that field and all its clovers.

Word

The next word I set down becomes a vivid mist
that rises from the page, drifts back in time
to enfold the awkward bearlike shapes
history has deposited, darkling and apart,
on the maps of memory.
                              Whatever was known
becomes unknown; whatever was defined
loses definition. Everything is shadow,
all shadow in a world of smoke.

With the next word I set down we shall
begin again.
                       The heavy fog of Forgetting
shall roll from horizon to horizon
like a sea composed of a single tear.

With the word I set down after
the next word I set down,
all is obliterate.
                          It becomes
a blind white plain as far as anyone can see,
a clean snowfield into which we march like children,
printing our fine new names.

Literature

The girls and flowers keep changing into literature
until that endless languid age arrives
when all the world becomes a picture catalogue of gardens
where men and women play at chess, at love,
and every animal comes fawning to the hand.

Then the spirit must begin once more,
untaming everything that it has tamed,
forgetting all that it has paid for in blood,
until the blazoned phrases melt from the vellum
and the gold-leaf initials turn into butterflies
and lift off the pages, climbing into space
to find the hidden planet all wild rose and chicory.

Slow signals are emitted from that far system.
The planet throbs in its orbit like a hive of sleepy bees,
the seasons settle into an undying summer
where poplar leaves slide in the wind
like shoals of rainbow trout nibbling the river.
It is a world prepared for men,

but no one comes, each reader still entranced
by the courtly chronicle of his native world,
the book that murmurs the secret names of lovers.

The Reader

for Helene

Beside the floor lamp that has companioned her
For decades, in her Boston rocking chair,
Her body asks a painful question of the books.
Her fingers are so smooth and white
They reflect the pages; a light
The color of cool linen bathes her hands.
The books read into her long through the night.

There is a book that opens her like a fan: and so
She sees herself, her life, in delicate painted scenes
Displayed between the ivory ribs that may close up
The way she claps the book shut when she's through
The story that has no end but cannot longer go.
It doesn't matter what the story means;
Better if it has no meaning—or just enough
For her to say the sentence that she likes to say:
Why do these strange folks do the way they do?

And yet they comfort her, being all
That she could never be nor wish to be;
They bring the world—or some outlook of its soul—
Into her small apartment that is cozy
As the huddling place of an animal
No one is yet aware of, living in
A secret corner of a secret continent,
An animal that watches, wonders, while the moon
Rides eastward and the sun comes up again
Over a forest deep as an ocean and as green.

The Garden

The garden is a book about the gardener.

Her thoughts, set down in vivid greenery,
The green light and the gold light nourish.
Firm sentences of grapevine, boxwood paragraphs,
End-stops of peonies and chrysanthemums,
Cut drowsy shadows on the paper afternoon.

Out of their hiding places the humid twilight
Lures the stars. The perfumes of the grass
Draw like cool curtains across the mind
And what the mind is certain it is certain of.

So that the twilight fragrances are clearly audible,
The garden stroking the senses with slow roses.
Bats ramble overhead, tacking from star
To early star as if putting in at ports of call.
And then the Chinese lantern is lit as it was in childhood,
As central in that place as an island lighthouse.

The gardener is a book about her garden.
She walks among these leaves as easy as morning
Come to scatter its robins and tender noises.
As the plants inhale the morning and its green light,
The book is open once again that was never shut.
What now we do not know we shall never know.

Proposition IVa.

This power exists and is bounded by no other power.

This music is conceived in and through itself.

Absurd to imagine this space affected by duration,
that is a false idea of those who conceive only dying things.

For if the one Rose were bounded by another rose,
we could not then call that first flower infinite.

It is impossible that it is not infinite.

It must then follow that this music has infinite substance
and that this substance has infinite attributes.

Our senses perceive only modes, but our intellects
perceive the attributes of the flower.

Each attribute is infinite and bounded by no other attribute.

Therefore the Rose is infinite
and infinitely expressed by the music.

For these reasons and for others that attentive minds will discover,
we have founded the City That Is a Garden
and established the worship of the Radiant Virtues.

Visitation

The ocean's blue smokes seize the capsized town,
the visions of drowned sailors overtake
the harbor and its sullen wares. *Mother,*
I thought of you when the hull stove in, when
the planet came round on my head like a moon
of pensive waters.
                    A rainbow oil slick
ribbons the current which the roar and slather
of storms confuse. The silent men spin down.

I feel like somebody has shipwrecked for me.
Who in the wind is calling to the sleepers?
The dark town's dreams whiten over the sea,
the lonesome streets shine wet in the last deep hours
before the sun climbs out of the smoke-blue
heartless morning. *Somebody, shipwrecked for me.*

Score

Something frozen is overtaking my soul,
Something dark. The blaze of afternoon
Whitens us into the wall
That seals the street off like a stone.
Perched on the flaking cornice a crow
Cocks up at a cloud. Rain
At twilight. Afterward, a row
Of orderly stars like punctures in a vein.

The midnight of the needle
And the nickel. The fairway suburbs send
Their homesick daughters out to wheedle
The howling stranger and habitual friend.
She delivers her snowy intelligence;
Her emptied eyes declare
A whole Manhattan of indifference,
A whole Miami of despair.

Teller

The money appears as jittery fireflies
Her black screen has netted. They suspend
A moment within their small abyss,
They tell their little story and go away.
Her computer circumspectly peeps; displays
New constellations of number without end,
Mint-green and cool and dry,
As fleeting and irrevocable as a kiss.

What an ardent gossip it is, this sleek machine!
Nothing but rumors of money the livelong day.
It tells her everything but where the money is,
Or if it really exists. Probably
It doesn't exist. It's only Business,
Something you have to take on faith to mean
Something. A ghost, like PERKINS, P T, whose name
Appears before her in letters of ghostly flame.

But isn't that the truth no one is telling?
The people don't exist, nor even the money.
No one is actually out there, only the box
Throbbing to its mates like a cricket.
That's why she feels so alone. It's funny
She never thought, except it's such a killing
Thought: Everybody lonely
Except the box which would like to feel lonely,
Or happy or bored or nostalgic—or downright wicked.

Dipperful

"Help yourself to a drink, it's toted fresh."

My hand rose in the water to meet my hand
And in its shadow his sweet spring appeared.
Mica-grains swarmed out of the hill-womb,
A funnel of sand trailed a crawfish.
I drank the hill. Scatter of sand-motes sparkled
When I launched the gourd's blind belly back in the bucket,
And on my tongue the green hill sprouted ferns.

Went back to jaw and ravel the afternoon
With the old man on his porch that shaded his hounds
Beneath, warm spotted lumps of doze and quiver.
I sat down easy. We sat and watched the cornfield
Across the creek get tall.

                   "Been walking far?"

"Not half as far," I said, "as my feet think."
He nodded and thumbed a twisted cigarette shut.
"Used to," he said, "I'd wear the daylight out,
I'd trudge till my cartridges was gone. I shot
To death I swear to God all the pokeweed
In Johnson's pasture. That would keep me going.
A boy'll walk to the end of the world, not thinking."

"Sure. But when you had to walk to work—"

"—They couldn't inch me along with a go-devil . . .
But if we didn't have the triflingness
To think back on, nobody would come this far."

"How far?"

                 "Seventy-five years this December."
He spat and watched it roll up in the dust,
Leaned back, and thought the thoughts an old man thinks.
I felt myself slide off the edge of his mind.
Dreaming, he spoke. "What hinders my sleep most
Is my daddy's boots. Seems like they come sailing
At me when I shut my eyes, bobbing

Off the floor by his bedside. Great heavy things
That felt as hard as iron when I was a youngun.
The way he kept them candled, rubbing and rubbing
At night to keep the water out, the way
The upper hooks would shine like a black cat's eyes.
I'd ponder on them, how strong I'd have to be
When I got growed to march my boots along.
Can't I just hear him puffing like when he'd bend
Over to lace them to the top? His hair
Flopped down on his face. He'd straighten up
And stare at nothing, at the day that was coming ahead.

"I remember one time I reached my hand in there.
Jerked it right out again. That surprised me,
How hot his boots got, hot as fresh ashes.
All day long the old man's walking in fire:
That's what I thought, and thought I didn't want
To olden and walk in fire the way he did.
And I don't know I did, the way he did.
I never got married, you see, never had
To grub for other people. I worked enough
To keep myself sufficient peace and quiet.
The world ain't all that lonesome for more MacReadies.
Now I'm so busted down there ain't much left,
But not a burden to some old muley woman."

He spat again and a swoon of flies unsettled,
Then settled back. The early afternoon
Began to climb the fields. "I've talked too much,"
He said. "I wish I didn't talk so much."
When he said that, the silence had its say.

Webern's Mountain

He felt the web of light unravel, rainbow
Filaments from point to point detach
And quiver to invisibility
Like a newly discovered harmonic system at mercy
Of the State. Like an edelweiss dissected
With a bayonet. He felt it coming apart,
All of it at once coming apart;
And the time drew on again to climb the mountain.

The air was diamond-pure at these thin heights
Where nobility was forgotten and created.
The true nobility of perfect freedom,
The perfect nobility of true Idea.
He loved the ledges where no accident
Was possible without inhuman disaster.

Sator arepo tenet opera
Rotas. *Keep the work circling,* keep the work
Contained, hermetic as fugue and involute
As the seashell lodged in the sky-lost precipice.
Might he not find among these terrible peaks
The flower that Goethe postulated, Ur-plant,
Theme for the infinite variations that greenly
Populate the world and all its mind?
The flower that from corolla to spidery root hair
Is but a single thought, a single wordchord.

Below the clouds the Fascists gathered their bundles
Of Jews and poets, preparing the clinical bonfire
That would cauterize the decadent suppuration,
Establish Ordnung for the blond millennia.

On Webern's mountain each row on row of rote tor
Was order consecrate by Origin,
Thematic figures etched upon a sky
That, arching, endlessly opened and enclosed it.

Then it came apart, the stave-line filaments
Of gleam snapped by mortar shell, viola

And cello strings dying under the tank treads.
And the lovely mountain fled to America,
The beautiful mountain that was Webern's father.

Epilogues

Caligari by Dreamlight

In the willow garden the silent wraith
drifts by like a lonely blot of steam.
Eyes like cigarette burns.

Now we plunge the cruel diagonals,
the ancient town layered like an artichoke.
Shadow sleeps on the skin of light.
Always some of us are mad,
sometimes all of us are mad.
There is one of us who never wakes.

Help help I am in the black box
Mouth stuffed with deadly truth
Another me who cannot speak

Within the gnawed book the secret crawls
like a silverfish; when the Doctor grins
darkness slathers the windows.

I carry over the rooftops my white bride.
I shall lie in my coffin with folded arms.
I will not do what you say.
Put the Doctor away.

Years Afterward

an epilogue to *The Wind in the Willows*

They're decades older now, and Time
Has brought its autumn change to Toad,
To Rat, to Mole. No more for them
The rigors of the Open Road,

Encounters colorful and strange
With every kind of Wayfarer.
They know they shall no longer range
So wide. Before his cozy fire

Mole sits his armchair, his feet up,
And listens to November wind
Puff his chimney like a pipe.
He reads his paper to the end.

Perhaps this evening Rat will come
For an unaggressive game of chess
And a crumb of gossip. And a crumb
Of Wensleydale and watercress.

Perhaps no one will come, and Mole
Shall spend the hours in reverie
While the wind dampens its raw brawl;
Then rise to brew a cup of tea;

Then sink into his chair again.
Those days of high emprise appear
With the May-wine freshness of spring rain
And paint their pictures in the fire.

So long ago . . . Now they all slip,
Abstracted, comfortable, and grubby,
Into old age. Though Toad has taken up
Hang gliding—as a sort of hobby.

Observers

after Einstein's *Relativity*

1

To time are added the three diversions of space:
these are the coordinates that allow us to say
Let us suppose

Let us suppose
an observer observing within this system
To him all things are systematic

Never can he know that he supposes merely:
the wherefore of his motions
he thinks he knows without supposing:

2

Yet all the consistent systems lie to one another:
the observers in their hurtling coordinates
are bound by treaty never to agree:

Because they cannot measure their separate measures:
the yardsticks shrink like accordions
the clocks contract toward yesterday

As the systems approach the friendly confines
of the speed of light, as the snail-shaped gravities
curl up in pain:

3

The separate systems veer together and apart:
the graffiti that their motions trace on space
we read as time:

It is not absolute:
the observers in their various systems
enjoy separate times and variously:

They are at rest with respect to nothing:
nothing in respect to anything is at rest:
Let us suppose nothing at rest we need ever to respect:

4

It is anyhow a universe,
the first in the history of this century,
a century collapsing like mass approaching c:

An era when anomalies flower into laws,
the laws give rise to lovely anomalies:
a time of arbitrary starlight

Which is drifting toward the place where Mozart
goes unheard forever, which is punctuated by
the blackened matchstem that was Nagasaki

Ideally Grasping the Actual Flower

after Kant's *Prolegomena*

1

Here is a gross and bumbly man, alas,
At large in the garden which perhaps he postulates.

In the indifferent space within him or beyond
Something appears that represents its name as *rose,*
Some shape that employs the gross and bumbly mind
To identify itself, a humoresque
Geometry that colors saturate,
That mortal perfumes burden and extend.

He has the impression of being unsatisfied.

2

He is unsatisfied, being one
Of the only class of beings that regrets its being.

Determined to picture this *rose* as pictureless,
He says, "It is a statement,
A mere location of possibilities
Which may remain unsatisfied."
Thus he can see (so far as he can see),
Requiring a mind as pure as the senses which feed it,
Demanding senses pure as spaceless time.

He moves upon the *rose* like a cloud of smoke
Attempting to envelope a puff of mist,
Ignoring the blandishment of metaphor
And the appetites of his rude sensorium.

He gives the impression of being satisfied.

3

The final possibility has been satisfied:
"I am a man alas and gross."

Now that even the numbers have stripped to their motives,
Now that the unquestioned authority of music
Is challenged by its smallest elements,
This *rose* begins to reckon its proper genus.

His flower is an angel.
The Rose is an Angel whose qualities
Are mathematic as a snowflake,
As empiric as the faultless Empyrean.

This truth comes to him as clear and poignant
As one's own porch light seen from a distant planet.

Subject Matter

an epilogue to Goethe's *Theory of Colors*

It is nice to imagine how Auden would open
a poem about the *Farbenlehre* with a genial phrase:
"The mistaken Faust put down his prism . . ."—
something like that, but defter; would find an *ism*
rhyme pleasant and refreshing, and with polished ease
would set the situation, drop in
an intriguing fact or two,
keeping in mind his aim to civilize
our anxious century.

He would range at will the plateaus
of Weimar culture, pause
to characterize some eager sycophant
like Eckermann, or to admire the earnest Schiller
(with witty reservations), pursue an elegant
allusion, squash an absurdity with a killer
epigram
and deal with irrefrangible Newton at the close
of his bookish poem

that seemed somehow not bookish at all.
Seemed instead a colloquy
in a dim-lit donnish study over a cup of tea
or an equivalent dose of gin while his stiletto
gaze sought the shadowed wall
behind you as he recalled to memory
Goethe's remarks on Tintoretto,
capitalizing with mock-Teutonic irony
words like *Modern Science* and *Sociology.*

You'd come away
believing you *knew* the book you hadn't read
half through, and that something had been said
that made the stubborn Ocean of the Past
whiffle with a bit of zephyr from Today
as the poet chatted. Taking leave at last,
you'd walk into the park and see a cloud
above a sunset tree reflect a purple ray
in just the manner Goethe understood.

And, as if walking off the edge
of a table, exit the city and its planet, leaving
behind the brandy and tobacco, the books, the wedge
of Stilton—all the smelly evening
comforts of the bachelor gender—and trudge
in hueless space
directly to the source
of light, where an endless sheet of stars
burns palpitant and interweaving.

Remodeling the Hermit's Cabin

an epilogue to the Constitution of the United States

Not what we expected. And dark in there,
The one little window not a proper window—
A chopped-out off-square page of cloud and treetop
That let a grayness in. No pin-up girls
Leggy in froth panties, but recipes
On the walls, head-heavy crayons of hawks,
Torn-out leaves of Bibles, pictures of flowers.
"This old feller was a different kind of lonesome,"
Reade said. We didn't understand. The bed
Was rusty and narrow. The floor was bare.

We found his handiwork. A carved and sanded
Walking stick with a twice-twined rattlesnake
Leaned in the corner. Ferrule and knob smeared silvery,
The snake was blotched unlikely black and orange.
Reade hefted it for balance. "I've seen worse,"
He said. "This old-time whittling, you always wonder
Where they got the hours. I bet I've started
A dozen, and never finished one I'd carry."

In a corner shelf we found his Little People,
Whittled men and women and children hand-sized,
Naked, or dressed in closely twisted cornshuck,
Disposed in attitudes forlorn and studied,
Each inhabiting a single space
That set it well apart from all the others,
Even in the narrow shelf. "His family,
How he remembers the way it was," Reade said.
"You see they didn't get along too good,
But what the story is would be a puzzle.
This one here is him." The only doll
He didn't give a face, an oval of soft
White pine blank as a thumbnail, a spindly figure
Turned toward the ragged chinked log wall, unclothed,
And set apart from the drama the other dolls
Absorbed themselves in, deaf or contemptuous
Of passions fierce for all their littleness,
Fiercer perhaps because of littleness—

A figure the world had cut no features on,
Musing the figureless wall that was his mirror.

We swept them all into a cardboard box.

Outside we gathered our courage. "That Florida buyer
Wants us to raise the roof," Reade said, "and lower
The floor. Might be we'll do the roof pretty easy,
Just loosen the nails and shim it up with blocks
Wedged in under the joists. But would you look
At them foundation beams? That main one there
Must be two-and-a-half foot square, and dug in
Solid where it's set two hundred years."

"Whose cabin was it before the hermit came?"

"Old hunting club from maybe nineteen hundred.
Before that I don't know—Daniel Boone's,
I reckon. Don't see logs like this no more."
He measured it with his tape. "What'd I tell you?
Thirty inches, and lodged into the hill
Since the flood of Noah."

                              "Well, what'll we do?"

"Rassle it," he said, "unless you've got
A better notion."

                    We wrestled it. And broke
The handles of two twelve-pound sledges, and bent
His faithful old black crowbar into a u.
We stopped for a cup of water from the s-
shaped runlet below the spring. "Takes a grade-a
Fool to take this ruinous job," Reade said.
"They could've paid us to cut a window or two
And left it like it was. There ain't no way
To get the foundation as stout as it used to be."

"What do you reckon it cost to build this cabin?"

"Twenty-eight dollars and twelve and one-half cents,
In pure cash money. Then you've got your labor,
And the brains it took to think the construction out,
And whatever it's worth to stand out independent
And be thought wild or crazy or just plain dumb."

"It looks kind of sad and busted, what we've done,"
I said.
      "That Florida feller will tack up plastic,"
He said, "and put him in an ice machine,
And have him a radar carport and a poodle
He's trained to count his money. These modern days
We're all a bunch of cowbirds, you know that?"

How the Job Gets Done

an epilogue to Lucretius

A dust of rubble warriors whitens the plain
where the chariots plunged and shattered. The sleep
of bronze and the noble memorial wind
caress those acres like a crop of wheat,

the rivers have carried away the mules flyblown
and bloated, the widows' torn veils,
the hafts and dented greaves, the portable gods.
Insubordinate Thersites got seven solid years

latrine duty no one is marking now, except
in his garden the poet who labors to line-end,
turns back like a sweating plowman to fold
another loamy furrow over the crumbled palaces.

Digs

an epilogue to *Beowulf*

1

The snow places
a cool feminine bandage on the graves
of thanes and chieftains. Night makes
its surgeon rounds among the grave-heaps.
The stars, a flock of mendicant widows,
gather to the vault of heaven, sing
the ritual lay with little frightened voices.

Dig here to find the ruined harp
embedded in blue clay. Over there,
a shield with cunning copper bosses.
Farther along the slope lie the bones
of an outcast cult, that patch
of soil set darkly apart.

This the vallation the Romans built
and died in before the eastern troubles
called them off these white headlands,
furrow where rude lovers
came to lie hungry at twilight.

Between the airport highway and the rail tracks,
the rubble of a dozen humdrum cultures.

2

Quite a triumph in the professor's notebook:
        the Beaker People
        the Corded Pot People
        the Long Knives
        the Beveled Knives
        the Earthworks People
        The graffiti of Bronze Age B
        remarkably modern in obscenity.

The millennia layered as precisely
as the strata of a Sachertorte.

Walk dazed out of the babble of artifacts
into a light like sword-clash.
We will take a familiar bourbon
and look out the motel window
into the snowy fields that lift around us
like footnotes submerging a page of text.
We will formulate a theory
of fine tedium, reinterpret all the potsherds.
Something will occur to us.

Something will recur to us.
The past opens out like a fan of river-delta;
the future narrows to a point of blackness
unsteady as the winter fly, the Last Survivor,
butting against the cold invisible pane.

3

Is it true the Goths rise out of our sleep
and stalk the corridors of this Holiday Inn?
The Goths, the Geats, the Frisians,
Helmings, Heathobards, Wulfings?

Someone pursues the nicors we dream
into dim glory, walks into sword-clash
like fierce sunlight.
     Those shaggy heroes
now the guardians of a race of clerks.

The clerks have been here before us.
Trace their footnotes through maze on maze
of stacks in the gloomy sub-basements
where horrid hypotheses flex their talons,
where many a scholar has secured his tenure
with a single deft citation.
      Ageless
snowfall of proud emendation.

From the highway now a psychedelic van
pulls into the parking lot
with an armory of new religions.

Scarecrow Colloquy

an epilogue to the Gospels

Ahoy, Ragwisp, how fares my Sentinel of the Stars?
Have you yet fixed for good the thrust of history?
I find you in the field as entranced as Saint Jerome.

I am glad, friend, of your company.
The man who nailed me up, left me to challenge
the courage of the crow, does he still thrive?
Or has this age of snow buried him beneath?

I know him of old, high Hayhead. What would you of him?
That he unfold the motive of your construction?
He being who he is can never say.

He is the hard farmer who maintains the fenceline.
He studies a-nights, the gleam of his window
gives a point to my musing. Let him come riddle me
from his big book the question and solution.

He knows you not, I tell you. He has forgotten.
The weeds and nettles of his field, his goats
and cattle, are all the business of his mind.

Does he never remember me ever?
When frost has stiffened my eaten coat, I seem to see him
rocking by the fire with his dreaming meerschaum
and thinking of his friend in God, the Scarecrow.

The toil of his flesh he knows, and when
the fields are silent asleep and his children asleep,
he ponders a matter you will not care to hear.

This autumn I have warded off the blackbird;
I have stood a steady watch while the stars went down;
I tallied the moons coasting over the stubble.
I have kept faithful till the seasons scattered.

O keep the faith, Chaffstaff, by any means.
This disaster they call a world might find a pivot
if you but stand outlined within the sunrise.

I have spoken in the field till my voice became an owl.
I have surveyed the horizon till I lost my buttons.
The fieldmouse heard my silence and gnawed my flesh of grass.
And still I stand here, guarding the bones of Adam.